Hold Your Own

Also by Kate Tempest

Brand New Ancients

Kate Tempest

Hold Your Own

B L O O M S B U R Y

NEW YORK · LONDON · NEW DELHI · SYDNEY

Bloomsbury USA
An imprint of Bloomsbury Publishing Plc

1385 Broadway
New York
NY 10018
USA

50 Bedford Square
London
WC1B 3DP
UK

www.bloomsbury.com

BLOOMSBURY and the Diana logo are trademarks of Bloomsbury Publishing Plc

First published by Picador in 2014
First U.S. edition 2015

ISBN: PB: 978-1-63286-205-1
ePub: 978-1-63286-206-8

LIBRARY OF CONGRESS CATALOGING-IN-PUBLICATION DATA
Tempest, Kate.
[Poems. Selections]
Hold your own : poems / Kate Tempest. —First U.S. edition.
pages; cm
ISBN 978-1-63286-205-1 (softcover)
I. Title.
PR6120.E655A6 2015
821'.92—dc23
2014045094

2 4 6 8 10 9 7 5 3

Typeset by Hewer Text UK Ltd., Edinbugh
Printed and bound in the U.S.A. by Thomson-Shore Inc., Dexter, Michigan

To find out more about our authors and books visit www.bloomsbury.com.
Here you will find extracts, author interviews, details of forthcoming events
and the option to sign up for our newsletters.

Bloomsbury books may be purchased for business or promotional use.
For information on bulk purchases please contact Macmillan Corporate and
Premium Sales Department at specialmarkets@macmillan.com.

For all of you, for all of it, but especially for India,
who taught me how to hold my own.

TIRESIAS: I will go, once I have said what I came here to say.

– Sophocles, *Oedipus Rex*

Contents

MANHOOD

BLIND PROFIT

Hold Your Own

Tiresias

Picture the scene:
A boy of fifteen.
With the usual dreams
And the usual routine.

Heading to school with a dullness inside
Borne of desires left unsatisfied.

Is he stifled or is he just
Learning the ways of his times?
Give him limbs that are awkward
But know how to climb.

Give him a gait that you know.
Give him hopes.
His days are so painfully slow,
But he copes.

This morning
He wakes to the same old alarm.
Slumps in the shower
Like a frog in the rain.
Winks at the mirror – does cool, does charm.
Shaves soft skin.
Nods at the pain.
No hair yet. Soon though.

Headphones on.
Last half of last night's joint in his lips.
Bass so loud it feels like a movie.
Scuffing his trainers.
Swinging his hips.

They're always laughing,
The kids at the bus stop.
He tries to ignore them,
But it doesn't help.

Hood up, he walks past them.
Blowing out smoke rings.
Singing out Wu-Tang.
Hating himself.

Into the woods, he takes the old path.

There is the rope swing,
There is the bath lying broken.
There is his name in the bark.
There are the trees,
So slim and so stark
In the thin little woodland.
Hardly a forest,
The last of the green washed clean by the grey.
There is the bike chain that nobody wanted,
There is a child's shoe
 – hope they're ok.

Out of the damp leaves and mulch in the pathway
His eye is caught by a glittering flash.
A dark moving something,
A mess of bright muscle.
Ore in a forge,
A deep, billowing gash.

Snakes. Two snakes!
Coiling, uncoiling
Boiling and cooling
Oil in a cauldron
Foil in a river
Soil on a mood ring.

He stares:
They spoil each other.
They do things
He has only dreamt of doing.

His blood's alive inside him, fizzing.
He shuts his eyes and watches blotches
Underneath his lids for minutes.
But peeks before he knows he's peeking.

Clutching his knees, he squats on his haunches
Watching the scales as they bounce and contort
And before he has thought he has reached out a fist
And picked up a short stick that lies near a ditch.

He swings from above
And breaks open the fortress.
The snakes, now apart,
Seem smaller, more awkward.
They flee for their love.
The boy, swaying and nauseous
Falls to the floor
More raw than before,
More tortured.

He feels himself shiver, contorting.
A current is coursing within him,
Shorting his circuits.
He curses,
His curses are perfect
The trees bow their branches in worship.

His body's responding to something beyond him.
Swells where before there were dips.
A crunching of muscle, the hips
Opening up, bones roaring,
Beneath them, boyhood shrinking, falling inwards.
Thinking nothing.
Feeling new blood rushing.

Scuffing ankles on the forest floor
As his shape moves
His body pours itself to puddles.
He fits and starts.
He will be more than the sum of his parts.
He shakes and shouts, a screwed-up mouth.
A pain that only women know
Grabs him in the guts.
He slows to gently stuttered breaths

He stops.
He feels.
He's still.
He rests.

And slowly, with caution
She climbs to her feet.
Wipes tears from her cheeks with her sleeve.
Frowns at the trees.
How could you stay so calm?
Places a nervous palm
Against her new face, her new chest,
The new flesh of her arm.

She approaches the school gates,
She can't face her class.
She can't go home, not now.

She is glass
Amongst sand.

She turns and retreats.
Finds herself deep
In the smog and the heat,
The fog and the meat
Of the bodies that beat out their lives
In the throb of the street.
She learns to be small and discreet.
She learns to be thankful for all that she eats.
She learns how to smile
Without meaning an inch of it.
She learns how to swim in the stink
And not sink in it.
It's as if this is all she has known.

Give her a face that is kind, that belongs
To a woman you know
Who is strong
And believes in the rightness of doing things wrong.

Give her a body that breathes deep at night
That is warm and unending; as total as light.

Let her live.

Brighter every day
That she was not so young and desperate.
Bigger every minute
That she settled all the restless
Urges in her chest
And when she woke from nightmares, breathless,
She would piece herself together
Like some relic found in ash and clay,
A precious, ancient necklace.

When she was complete again,
She'd wolfwalk into town.
And drink down every wave that came
To break her spirits down.
She was wild and wonderful.
A star throughout the district.
A red light dreadnought.
Queen among misfits.

And yes, sometimes they sneered
When they glimpsed her in the gutter.
It made her crack her knuckles,
Shake her head and start to mutter
To herself under her breath
You posh pricks don't know fucking shit.
And they would look away
And light their cigarettes and spit.

She liked to giggle with the pretty boys and kiss the lonely addicts
And weave exquisite curtains for the dismal little attics
Where they lay their heads at night,
Out of beads and string and plastic.
Each corner she inhabited made warmer by her magic.

She grew expert in the field
Of love
She learned to see and feel
The deepest secrets lurking in
The hearts of those who came to swim
In her dark waters.
She knew things.
She knew Kings
And she bore daughters.
She knew love, she made her fortune.
Till she met her match.
Exhaustion.

He was an older man,
A man who liked to hold her hand
A man who made her feel like she was rolling round on golden sand.

A man as soft as any girl
A man as hard as any luck.
She understood what life was for
Each time they bucked and came unstuck.

True love takes its toll
On souls
Who are not used to feeling whole.

They tangle limbs and feel the shudders,
All the world is nothing.
Lovers:
Promising each other not to take the vital parts,
While even as they mutter it, they're giving up their hearts.

It is a new moon
In late May
She gives way
To his weight
They are laid out flat by a lake.

She can feel
His blood in her veins.
He can feel
Her pulse in his wrists.
And they kiss.
And the moon hangs open and orange
Like a wound in the mist.

He asks her to marry him.
Have him forever and never be lonely but only together.
She thinks that he's taking the piss.
Throws him a scowl so sharp his darkest parts are shafted, blasted,
    ripped in half,
She starts to laugh, she hits her palms
Against the grass. He lifts his arms, *I mean it*
Shining cheeks, his garments creased,
Naked skin on cold damp heath. *I mean it.*
Silence. Let it land.
She cannot breathe or stand.
She crawls towards him, smiling.
Takes his hand.
Of course.
They kiss and both expand.

She decides she must go back,
Seek out a past.
A mother, a father,
Whatever she has.
A blessing or something,
Maybe an answer.

She packs some things and leaves at dawn, alone.
And heads out North. For home.

By dusk she's walking the woods of her youth,
Smelling the air.
Is this where I'm from?

Who was I when I was here last?
If this isn't home
Then where has home gone?

She sees a small clearing between the trees.
She's rocks in a river.
She's leaves in a breeze.

There is a shopping trolley
There are some keys
There is a hawthorn
There's a horse chestnut
There's a used condom
There's an old desk lamp
There's a nice conker . . .
Is that blood or ketchup?
Birds in the branches
Light in the darkness
Like sand in the toes of the bushes.

There!

Right there.

There in the path. In the leaves and the bracken
Two black backs untangle, dragons.
Coupling, shuffling, grappling.
She is staggering.
Can't stop looking. Strange unravelling.
Something from before, something forgotten.
Someone she used to be.
Some rotten something in her darkest somewhere,
Scale and danger.
Nature, sunglare.
Faint, she takes a branch and holds it
Steadies herself. Stills her shoulders.
Snakes and sex and innocence
And nothing really makes much sense.

Who was I then?
She watches awed.
And grips the branch like it's a sword.

Believing.
Believing.

I should be leaving.

She breaks the branch with sudden force.
She swings the branch, and knows its course:
The snakes, no chance, are soon divorced.

A sudden dark and squelching tension.
She panics, sweats, can't breathe. Head pounds.
Her body writhes and juts.
No sounds.

The image of her lover's face
Begins to shake and wilt and fade,
She loses him, there, in the shade.

It hurts. She's felt this once before.
She knows this pain, this change, this awe.

She feels herself retract and harden.
Feels her bones enlarging,
Moving, arching.
Something charging,
She's old milk bursting from its carton.

Shaken, floored, a body heaving
Writhing, smiling, something's pleasing,
Finding her throat open, screaming,
Hoarse and full of light
Her body stops. She feels his might.
His veins thicken in intense delight.

A man again.
He stands, confused.
And walks away.
Too much to lose.

This poor once-boy, sudden-woman,
Who'd lived so long and done so well
And kept so much so deeply hidden,
Now found himself before the bell
Of some new door in some new town.
The pain of new beginnings.
Everything that went before
Gushed in him.
Water overfilling.

Smash the cup and let it happen.

Tiresias.
A full grown human.
Moves on from what he cannot fathom.
He swears his past will not consume him.

And so the man with many pasts
Matures into his present,
But he feels his waters move
In the last arc of the crescent,
And as the moon expands to full
He feels his blood respond,
But as all humans know to do,
He holds it in
And soldiers on.

Imagine how it feels
To walk so far away from life and love,
To know that all you've known
Is now
No longer enough.

All the blood they'd bled,
All the children they had borne,
All the mouths their mouths had met,
Behind them now.

Forlorn,
He staggers knee-deep through his pity
Sadness grabs his shins.
A stranger in a strangers' city,
Where new strangeness begins.

In distant god terrain,
Mount Olympus, pink and milky,
Zeus and Hera fight again,
Raw and honest, foul and filthy,
Hera with her eyes screwed up
I swear you're out to kill me.
She weeps and screams and he enjoys
The feeling of his power.
He froths and paces, thunders, pleads;
Tempers frayed, their bodies need
A break from fighting –
But none comes.
Not after this – another tongue
Roasted in his total blaze.
Surprise surprise, old Zeus has strayed.

The fighting carries on for days.

Down on Earth the weather's mental.
Hurricanes and ancient heat.
Sudden freezes ice the deserts.
Rain leaves craters in concrete.
Hera's ripping up her dresses.
– *Am I not enough for you?*

Zeus is melted, stares intently
– *Sister, you are all I love.*
– *Then why?*
– *Because these others tempt me.*
And unlike you, I lack the guts
To turn away and know my path.

Hera swigs straight from the cask,
The nectar's strong and soothes her heart.
She sighs in disbelief, *don't start.*

Zeus, bored of being wrong and sorry,
Puffs his chest up, shows his might.
Hera knows his godly body
Well enough to not take fright.

I don't know what the fuss is for
Zeus begins, playing wounded.
Women like it more than Men.
I don't even want to do it.
What you get from me is more
Than what I get from you.

Red rag to a Minotaur.

What? says Zeus. *It's true.*

They row like it's a holy war,
The Earth suffers their anger.
Finally, when neither has
The strength to raise the anchor
And the ship of their relations
Is broken-keeled and sinking,
And they're fighting over what the other
Might have just been thinking,

They stop for ragged breaths.
The sky is bruised and black.
Hera won't be pacified
Until he takes it back.

Tiresias, at peace at last,
Is older now than ever,
He's found a lovely partner
And they've made a life together.
He won't walk the woods alone;
He'll only walk the heath.
He blanks out all the lives he's known,
But they survive beneath.

He's started doing pottery.
He's joined the local choir.
If he thinks about his history
His heart is set on fire.

There's no way back,
There is no track
That leads to his past lives.
He sets himself on forwards.
And he loves.
And he survives.

His lover is a gentle man,
Together they are free.
They enjoy each other
I love him. And he loves me.

But on dark days he likes to walk
Beside the heartsick sea.
And as the waves begin to howl
He drops down to his knees,
And cries for all he's lost
And for all he used to be.

Zeus – in final stage of fury –
Beats his massive fists
Against the stormy clouds
And says – *there's only one who can fix this.*

Tiresias is home alone,
His partner's out all day;
He teaches in the local school
Good students but shit pay.

The weather's turning nasty
The house rattles and moans.
The door's ripped from its hinges
And Tiresias is thrown.

The house is filled with stormclouds
Rain smashes at his cheeks
He is too shocked to recognise
That this is how god speaks.

Suddenly the storm abates
The house is filled with sun
Zeus, in his human form,
Sticks up a golden thumb,
Hey.

Tiresias is terrified.
He can barely speak.
Zeus nods in recognition.
Swans in, takes a seat.

Look, me and Hera
Are having this domestic,
Pathetic — I know.
But that's what's to be expected
From an eternity of marriage.
Anyway
You're my only hope.

And Zeus takes him by the hand
— might as well have been the throat —
And ascends the mount Olympus
And dumps him before the queen.

Here's the guy to settle it.
Tiresias has been
Man and woman both.

So ask him *— who enjoys it more?*
A woman or a man?

Tiresias is stunned
But wants to help them if he can.

His mind begins to shudder,
Every kiss comes back to bite him.
His body buckles under
The old echoes of excitement.

He sees every time his open mouth has yelled,
All tongue and teeth,
He sees the necks and backs and legs,
His rising chest, his blushing cheeks.
He remembers after sex,
The woman he once was,
Lying in her happiness
Like nothing had been lost.

He thinks of how he finds it now,
Spent and drained and breathing deep.
The agony that follows.
The desperate need for sleep.

He feels it moving like a hand
Across his shaking thighs.
He takes his time and works it out,
And slowly he describes:

If you could split sexual
Pleasure into tenths,
Women would get nine.
That leaves just one
For men.

Zeus grins,
Smug,
In that way he does.
And Hera feels the boiling of her blood.

She, in rage and consternation,
Screams towards Tiresias
Takes the eyes out from his head
And leaves him blind and sore and red.
And gore is pouring forth before them all.
His arms are spread.
He wishes with his broken heart
He could be someone else instead.

Zeus is shocked, appalled, impressed.
Mate he says *Ah mate.*

Tiresias knows better
Than to howl and remonstrate
But his swollen eyeballs roll in grief;
His face is aged with pain.
Zeus, still reeling from his victory,
Accepts it is a shame.

What one god has done,
No other god can undo.
I can't give you back your eyes
But I can give you something new.

Zeus lays a mighty palm
Against the bloody sockets
And floods the body's blindness
With the inner sight of prophets.

Tiresias was melted,
But inside the vision grew.
A weakness in his legs,
A sobbing emptiness, shot through
With some new tenderness,
Some blue
And calm uncurling in his guts.

He staggered like a child pretending blindness,
Hands out in the dark.
But couldn't close his eyes to what exploded in his heart.
He could see the truth of things
He couldn't look away.
Nothing left but to accept,
He had been born to live this day.

And so, with face streaked warpaint red,
And every sense burnt white with pain,
He was given seven lifetimes
And dropped back down to Earth again.

A whole life lived
At the mercy of the fates.
Here he comes again,
The old seer with the shakes.
Wheeled on to mutter prophecy,
Chased off by angry kings.

Tiresias, you lived for more
Than what the legend sings.

Tiresias – you've lost
Everyone you ever loved.
But you stand beneath
The cruelty of the sun that burns above
And you offer only toothless grins
For all that you have seen.

Tiresias, you hold your own.
Each you that you have been.

You walk among us, slow,
A ragged crow,
With breath to blow,
In which we'll see a truth
That we'll wish we didn't know.

You're the crazy on the corner
Old, and smelling weird
Queuing for electric
With birdbones in your beard.

You stagger on regardless,
Swaying in the street
Summoning an oracle
That can't be arsed to meet.

While we assemble selves online
And stare into our phones,
You are bright and terrifying,
Breath and flesh and bone.

Tiresias – you teach us
What it means: to hold your own.

CHILDHOOD

TIRESIAS: You long for knowledge;
           you will soon long for ignorance.

– Euripides, *The Phoenician Women*

For my niece

I hold you in my arms,
your age is told in months.

There's things I hope you'll learn.
Things I'm sure that I learned once.

But there's nothing I can teach you.
You'll find all that you need.

No flower bends its head to offer
teaching to a seed.

The seed will grow and blossom
once the flower's ground to dust.

But even so, if nothing else,
one thing I'll entrust:

Doing what you please
is not the same

as doing what you must.

I was so much older then,
I'm younger than that now

It roars. Precious and hot and before time.
We played games on the alleyway railing.
I was the fat one. Good-natured and kind.
They were my friends. The world was our plaything.

We climbed hills to bury things. We drew maps.
Pulled our feet from the suck of the Quaggy.
Rules were if you flinched they got two free slaps.
My specs were large and my clothes were baggy.

Collected things that we found on the ground.
Always the goalie. I never complained.
I told the stories; they did the sounds.
We painted potatoes whenever it rained.

Snakes in the grass

I was walking my dog in the park.
He ran down to the wooded bit where I wasn't allowed on my own
and I followed him, calling.

I was a kind-hearted child. I'd run across the road to save a spider.
I glimpsed the top of his tail and clapped my hands.
I found him!

He was sniffing another dog.
The other dog was sat beside a couple lying down.
They didn't have their clothes on.

I dropped to my haunches to talk about dogs.
He was above her.
His elbows dug into the grass.

She was scowling at me,
her hair was long and sweaty.
They were wrapped in a cream blanket.

I stroked their dog.
Asked for his name.
Explained that some of my best friends were animals.

He told me to Fuck off.
It was the first time I'd heard it.
He hissed it full of venom and his eyes were black as 8balls.

Girl next door

I was seven,
my neighbour was eight.
She stuffed a pair of socks down my pants
and straddled me and called me big boy.

I didn't have a clue what it meant
but I've been dizzy on that feeling ever since.

Thirteen

The boys have football and skate ramps.
They can ride BMX
and play basketball in the courts by the flats until midnight.
The girls have shame.

One day,
when we are grown and we have minds of our own,
we will be kind women, with nice smiles and families and jobs.
And we will sit,
with the weight of our lives and our pain
pushing our bodies down into the bus seats,
and we will see thirteen-year-old girls for what will seem like the first
    time since we've been them,
and they will be sitting in front of us, laughing
into their hands at our shoes or our jackets,
    and rolling their eyes at each other.

While out of the window, in the sunshine,
the boys will be cheering each other on,
and daring each other to jump higher and higher.

Bully

I was sat beside her on the bench.
It was lunchtime and the boys were all playing football.
The girls sat on benches beside the field
and watched the boys.
Every now and then she'd grunt and say things like
cor I wouldn't mind having him

She'd had her period,
she said it was like being sick out your minge.
And she'd been fingered
and she had spots
and she knew swearwords
and she had boobs
and she gave blowjobs.

Before I had music and rhyming,
I was too big and I walked like a boy,
and I was too soft for the school that I went to
and I was too smart and it made her suspicious.
I had to be tenderised.

In the changing room,
girls sprayed so much Innocence it made the air toxic to breathe,
and brushed each other's hair
and sang pop songs.

The bully would point at my crotch
and ask what I had.
And I wouldn't understand
but I would blush and blush and blush.

Her sidekick was skinny and not very smart
and had hair like a short lampshade
and every time a boy walked past the bully would shout
shut your legs you minger, I can smell your dirty fanny
and the sidekick would stare at the ground.
Their mothers had been friends since they were at school.

School

We wander into school, happy children;
kind and bright and interested in things.
We don't yet know the horrors of the building.
The hatred it will teach. The boredom it will bring.

Soon we'll learn to disappear in public.
We'll learn that getting by is good enough.
We'll learn the way it feels to see injustice,
and shut our mouths in case it comes for us.

We'll learn to never think but copy blindly.
To ally with the mean and keep them near.
We'll learn to not be talented or clever,
and the most important lessons
for success in a career:

How to follow orders when you're bordering
on nausea and you're bored and
insecure and dwarfed by fear.

Sixteen

They think we're bad kids.
We have nothing but fury and bass
and dead friends that keep us close to each other.
We're tied to our fate like it's mythical.
But nothing is certain.

I'm a talented thief.
I push trolley loads of fancy booze out the doors of Tesco's
with a smiling nonchalance that makes me famous.

My family are worried.
Me and my dad are fighting with our hands.
My sisters can't reach me.
I've stopped coming home at night.
I've dropped out of school to sit around and laugh at people.

Waiting in the pool room for the Triad with the coke,
walking through the rain with a bar of hash strapped to my chest,
I feel like punching every stranger in the face.
My friends pass me the laughing gas.
When other kids throw parties, they hope that we won't come.

When I meet her, she is just like me.

I wake before her and start drinking.
She sees me at the foot of her bed,
smoking skunk out of her window,
watching all the chaos come to life below us.
And she whispers things I've never heard a person say.

When we walk down the street holding hands
grown men stuff theirs down their jeans and stare openly.
Groups of boys follow us to ask her why she's with me.
When we stand kissing at a party,
a man we've never met
grips the back of both our heads
and sticks his tongue into our mouths.

When the rumours start
I don't believe them.

Before her there were things that I trusted.
But now there is a loneliness so deep it sends me foetal.
And dark endless raves where she makes us both a spectacle
and all I want are the friends I've lost,
the certainty of knowing I have nothing.

The cypher

A circle. Shoulders and hard chests and arms like rosary beads
from push-ups before bed, eyes narrowed.
We wear our hoods up. We talk in couplets.
Two lines at a time and my heart has
never been calmer than here,
in the cypher.

I stare at my trainers and listen to deep voices
throwing out lyrics through smoke.
I know I can do this much better than them.
I can feel it. Something like stillness,
but nothing like stillness.

It creeps up my throat like water creeps down it.
It spreads itself over my tongue.
My shoulders are squared.
I move like the boys,
I talk like the boys,
but my words are my own.

And when I unleash them, my eyes widen and focus.
The streetlights stop flickering, just for a moment,
the arrogance prickles like sweat at my temples,
I'm moving as if I have never been gentle.
The kinder among them look at me sideways.
Smiling, shaking their heads,
I feel it all through me.
It's shaking my legs.

I push my fist against theirs, my soft arms are clasped,
I'm embraced like a man, my back slapped,
and my heart all the time getting faster.
The beatboxer nods his respect.
And I'm feeling bigger than
all of these buildings.
I wait for my turn again,
everything burning.

Age is a pervert. Youth is a fascist

Youth hates age, age loves youth.
This means we are born for unhappiness.
This means we will keep buying outfits.

Youth, in his hard-bodied, glistening bullshit
stares at the sagging mouths of his elders
and feels utter disgust and it makes him annoyed.

Why aren't they ashamed of themselves?
His youth is his victory, he wins every day that he's young.
He beats people up when he's bored.
He sniffs cheap drugs and plays with his balls in the classroom.
He can't stand ugly people.

When he steps out onto the street,
everyone is speaking his language.
He feels like the first to have ever done anything.

Age stares with dismay at Youth.
He'd shared that same air once
but now, he stands alone on the high street,
his glasses steamed up,
pulling his saggy pants out of his arsecrack.
When he thinks back, his entire life is movie stills.

He watches the arrogant arc of that young skull,
the swing of those young limbs and feels his guts drop.

If he could hold something young
just for a few good strokes

The boy Tiresias

Watch him, kicking a tennis ball,
keeping it up,
the boy on the street in his sister's old jumper.
Watch him,
absorbed in the things that he does.
Crouched down,
observing the worms and the slugs.

He's shaping their journeys
placing his leaves in their paths,
playing with fate.
Godcub.
Sucking on sherbet.
Riding his bike in the sunlight.
Filmic.
Perfect.

But one day
he'll be hunch-backed, riddled with pain.
Desperate for love but too weak to enjoy it.
Mumbling at strangers on trains, *how strange
that when we have youth we're so keen to destroy it.*

We do not choose
but follow blindly.
We do not own
just sometimes carry.
We do not make.
We undertake
to be more alive
each day we wake.

And this is a must.
And the days are all dust
and the only thing worse
than losing the trust
of a lover is finding the rust
in their kiss.

He will live longer than all of his passions.
But for now, he is young still, and everything's his.

Because the boy will grow up
makes him no less innocent.

Watch him,
staring at what doesn't bore him.
Sun of himself. All things are his moons.

He can even now
feel his destiny calling.
He holds it to his chest,
like a dressing to a wound.

Womanhood

Tiresias: The truth with all its power lives inside me

– Sophocles, *Oedipus Rex*

The woman the boy became

Born more brawn than most,
Born warm.
Born close to ghosts.
Born storm.
Born old.
Grew young.
You could tell she wasn't from
The same place as the rest,
Born strong.
Born wrong.

She grew.

Growing is what anyone would do.
Given the particulars
She knew what she knew
She was ridiculous.
Born too smart and too dumb.
Born to hold the world under her tongue.

Don't swallow yet.

She felt

All the things that others didn't feel,
Or if they did,
They did a lot to conceal what the feelings were.

She felt skies and bricks and rain.
She felt it all
It made her fall
And weep beneath a crawling dawn
When everything was ruined; torn.

She felt ill.
But she felt still.

How many *yous* have you been?
How many,
Lined up inside,
Each killing the last?

How many times have you
Seen yourself change,
Felt yourself splitting in half?

When does it happen? There in the moment?
Or when you look back and say
– that's when my changing began?

Born hero.
Born freak. Born weirdo.

Born blind.
Born seeing.

Born man.

She stands.

The hillside beneath her is crumbling.
The sky frowns.
The land wants to return to the sea.

She is food for the gulls and it's humbling.
But this is not all
That she was born to be.

All of the things in her life that have happened.
All of the changes.
All of the strangers.

All of the nights and the days in her heart
Have been present in her since the start.

You don't learn.
You remember.

Born with it all in your chest.
Born first.
Learn last.
Burn fast like paper
Unless you're wet logs.

Wet dogs shelter in her caves when they get lost.
Howl with her.

She has been touched without asking.
Punched by a madman.
Drunk in a bad town.
When she puts her hands down
And feels what's beneath
She feels all the grief
Of the world.
Lay a wreath
For the girls.

She will march
Till she feels the tarmac respond.
She will die for our wrongs.
We won't notice.

She is fire
And sleet and granite,
Space rock shattering the planet.
She wants to stop it spinning in its tracks like a dumb child.

She will be prophet one day.
For the moment
She soaks up all that she can
She will own it
This filthy body this life
The dethronement of all that was precious
In favour of all that is tepid.
Opponents mean nothing. She's Titan.
Born of the first breed.
Born in the last days.
Frightened of nothing that bleeds.
The more that you hate her
The less that she needs.

All of her childhood passed in a flash
When she woke on her back in a clearing.
Time to be me now.

How many *yous* will you carry,
Weeping and desperate to marry?
How many *yous* will you churn out?
Turn out the light for the night.
She has burned out but she'll be alright.
She is coming up.
Child of her time.

Red morning.
Blood on the tips of the thorns,
And the awning is dripping
With all of our scorn. We were born in
Days that will fill you with porn and with boredom
Grey little faces march in the squadron to warsongs
Penned by cynical fiends,
The latest big hit that cements the routine.
Sell us the download.
And kill all our dreams.

She rises.
She will see through the disguises.
They stab knives in her thighs.
See the swell of her iris?
She survives.
She will run till the cities are vanquished.
And all of the children are gods again.

On Clapton Pond at dawn

The pond was calm
the sky was new
your voice was soft your lies were true.
You were me and I was you
and I was going blind with you.

You told me I reminded you
of Venus when I smiled at you,
or angels that go flying through
the paintings in the quietest rooms
of galleries. Renaissance girls,
all soft curves and floating curls.
We sat there and the light shone through
the leaves and we admired the view.

I loved you.
I had died for you
that night,
I'd closed my eyes
and through the gaps
I'd sought your silhouette.
I'd given up my mind for you.
We did what all our kind would do.

You sat beside me, finding new
ways to look away.
You kissed me. It was lighter fuel.
It burnt the night away.
And when I took my eyes off you
I saw that it was day.

India

It was quite funny really.
We sat round the kitchen table,
a sisterhood,
drinking vermouth.

I opened the window,
blew my smoke into the night,
passionately drunk.
In love with two women and playing charming as hard as I could.

At some point
I asked you to carve your name into the flesh of my arm
with the blade of a Stanley knife.

You asked was I sure.
I said yes I was.
Looked at you and nodded deeply.
You were excited
in the way that you get
when things are unusual.
And so you pressed the blade in and you drew blood
and it hurt like everything hurt with you.

I smiled winningly
and bled everywhere.

The other woman I was in love with
filled my open wound with ink
and together
you rubbed fag ash into the bleeding letters.
Smiling at each other.
And at me.

I didn't realise it would last forever.

Now I wear your name in capitals across my right arm
and people think I found myself in Goa.

Remembering the way you kissed me once

You were driving, my legs were across your lap.
I rolled your cigarettes while you rubbed your hand over my ankles,
and picked my foot up by the sole
to kiss in between my toes with your tongue
and I giggled as if I was a beautiful girl.

And as you sucked my toes and drove the car,
I dared myself to focus on the side of your face.

In other cars, on other roads, in other towns,
I'm sure other lovers were glancing sideways,
smiling like morons, pushing their thighs down into their seats,
but none had the stop of blood,
the fall and crush and emptying that I had, right then.

Some couple

There's always some couple
in ravenous stages of loving
just when we've argued ourselves into cunts.

We'll be fuming,
walking along, saying nothing,
when suddenly,
here they come, skipping in front –

whispering,
smiling,
tickling,
cooing,

it makes me feel
empty
and angry
and dead.

But when I look at you
silently screwing

I know
I'd much rather
have this love instead.

The old dogs who fought so well

It struck me that morning. I was in Ireland, terrified in a tiny tent.
Outside, a storm was gathering gale force and I was going out of my mind
   with the guilt.
The drugs had made a monster out of my face.
In my head I was listening to Chopin and I was reading Joyce and I was
   in love with them for being so human and for saying it all so well.
I felt myself shrinking and desperate and worthless and I wondered if
   they ever felt like the most alone and despicable people in all of
   Poland, or Paris, or Dublin, or the World.
I could see him, Chopin – thin and pale at his piano stool, sicker every
   day, watching his hands getting older.
I could see Joyce, tearful behind his eyepatch – throwing himself into it
   in a room as dark as wet earth and I smiled to myself, and stopped
   trying to sleep.
The wind was still making an orchestra out of the tent. But it wasn't
   a requiem anymore.
Three mornings later, I woke up and reached for one of the books by
   the bed.
It was Bukowski. I opened him at random and read a poem I'd not read
   before – it was called *How To Be A Great Writer* and in it he said:

remember the old dogs
who fought so well:
Hemingway, Celine, Dostoevsky, Hamsun.

if you think they didn't go crazy
in tiny rooms
just like you're doing now

without women
without food
without hope
then you're not ready

And I laughed out loud. Because it's always the way – when you're alone
and feeling like you could jump off the edge of the world,
that's when they find you and tell you they all went through the same
thing.
And it makes you feel special because you feel like of all the people in all
the world, these yearsdead writers wrote whatever it was that made
the blood run in your veins again, just for you.
And you say their names out loud when you walk the city in the middle
of the night, and you feel close to something timeless;
you feel like someone just lay you down on your back and showed you
the sky.

What we lose

When I was young
I could speak to animals,
these days
I don't know what to say.

They used to sniff my ears,
but now
they smell my fear
and walk away.

You eat me up and I like it

The air is wet with pressure.
You stare at me across the table.
I feel like if I move
It will begin to rain.
You pile your fork and smile through mouthfuls.
Overwhelmed, I lean across to press my smile against your chewing lips.

The first thing I noticed about you was your lips;
Shaking with pressure.
Capable of mighty mouthfuls.
I gave you my hand. All my cards were on the table.
When we stood in the storm by the river, I couldn't tell your kisses from
    the rain.
We kept still and let the planet move.

It was your move.
You raised your eyebrows and licked your lips.
My clothes were cold skin from all the rain.
You grabbed me with so much pressure
Your fingerprints stayed on my arms after you'd gone, like tea stains on a
    coffee table
And my body shone all over from where you'd had your mouthfuls.

You say my name in between mouthfuls.
I feel you feeling me move.
The books, the lamp, the whisky all come crashing off your bedside table.
I bite down until I can taste blood on my lips.
We tried to play it cool. We promised *no pressure*.
But I couldn't keep myself from falling. Like the rain.

I lay in the dark and listened to the rain.
Drank the night in breathless mouthfuls.
The sky hung low and gave in to the pressure.
I stared at your back, desperate for you, trying to make you move.
But you were busy, chain smoking, swinging those legs off the edge of
    the table
And I could feel myself burning up each time the butt met your lips.

I watch your profile, the stretch of your nose, the curve of your lips.
The walls are the colour of rain.
I am jealous, territorial, stalking the pool table.
Swallowing drugs in clammy grey mouthfuls.
Eventually, you move.
On the jukebox, *Under Pressure*.

The train was full of people. I looked out at the rain and watched
    everything move.
You smiled tiny, wet mouthfuls out of my neck, lay a coat across our laps
    and did it to me underneath the table.
I couldn't take the pressure. Your eyes were bright with guilt. I saw the
    smile before it reached your lips.

Fuck the poem

I haven't written in ages
'cause I'd rather stare at you than stare at pages.

But what would be great is
making a poem that could be half as courageous
as you when you're naked.
I try for a minute –

Your love is my metal, your kisses my rivets.
You are like the ocean beneath the slick of a spillage.

Fuck the poem.

There's a bed here
and you want me in it.

Waking up with you this morning

You yawn. I watch your chin obey your mouth
through eyelids not yet sure that I'm awake.
Small creases gossip softly on your face.
The warmth you emanate will heat this house.

I watch you coming back from where you've been.
It clings to you. Your naked shoulders glow,
catch dawn and hold it still and make it slow.
Your eyebrows play your dreams through scene by scene.

You burrow down then climb up laughing, squash me,
your hungry kiss-mouth wanting to be fed.
Slow and soft, you spread yourself across me
your lips lead mine like needles leading thread.

Sometimes I catch a glimpse and I'm amazed:
I've seen you but not looked at you for days.

The woman Tiresias

At first she was worried, of course.
Dragged her shape around like chains.
Was it real or was it magic?
She watched herself in the windows of traffic.
Heard the drivers call her darling.

She threw herself into the rituals.
Manned the tills for bed and victuals.
Worked like she was born to work
And soon she felt, as we all feel,
That if it's happened, then it's real.

What a body's for in times like these
Is yours to guess or know.
Her body was a new and ancient rite
She felt her wanting grow.
But could not reconcile her wants
With what she knew she was.
She let herself be touched
But not for pleasure. Just because.

New flesh for old,
She learned her limits and controlled
Her deepest fidgets.
She sought wealth to lift her up.
Could not rest with feeling stuck.
Getting by is fine for some
But she was after better luck.

Sitting in the finest winebars
Sipping from a shining wineglass
She remembers ancient times
When she was young, a boy who climbed
On top of girls to feel them grind.
And how she fought so she could find
Herself top boy. Those days, divine.
All tough and raw and caked in grime.

Those days are in her, howling still,
Yes, she's calm and humble now,
But that dark music, wild and shrill
Still plays each time the night comes down.

Those days still follow her around
Stagger leering through the streets
Growling at her, gaining ground,
While she unwraps the posh pink sweets
From suitors who mistake her charms
For something strange they'd like for theirs.
Those simpletons who think they dance
A step that no one else has shared.

Her body smarts, she grits her teeth,
How many of us must we be?
She knows that she is full of something
New and foul and deep and free.

The boy in her is strong some days
And calls out for a girl to touch
The girl in her is full of rage
And craves the things she hates so much.

She must be more than sex and body?
Sex and body's all she's got.
Like all hard lessons, learn it softly.
It only is until it's not.

Manhood

TIRESIAS: All men make mistakes, it is only human.
But once the wrong is done, a man
Can turn his back on folly

– Sophocles, *Antigone*

The man Tiresias

It came out of nowhere.
All teeth and tussle.
Shouting like huge crowds behind him.

It stamped on his bones.
It shovelled his muscle.
Alone in a clearing where no one would find him.

He writhed in its jaws:
his lovers flashed past him.
The routine, the dinners, the dishes.

He felt the dense forest
close in and enchant him.
Cleansed of his longing for kisses.

He rose like a wreck on a winch.
Swaying and derelict.
Suddenly boy again. Soon to be man.

All of his grief was a burden to keep
deep down in his guts.
And he turned and he ran.

Fighting with shadows.
Swinging at birds as they laughed.
Too shaken to hate what had happened.

All that he'd learned to be true
fell to pieces.
He stared at the sun till it blackened.

Watching his body like it wasn't his.
He pushed his new shape
to the edge of the clearing.

And found the red road
that led out of the city.
And screamed until no one could hear him.

He journeyed for days,
until he was purified.
Feasting on tree bark and roadkill and petrol.

Macho man; ate cars for breakfast.
Natural man; skin the same texture as cactus.
Hands grew wild and dextrous and flew at his side like two kestrels.

His feet became tougher than limpets
his eyes became keener than knives,
his breath melted padlocks.

He heard a leaf falling
from five miles away,
and he moved like a dog on a ham hock.

All knowledge was his
and he learned the old words
for the things that he saw. He spoke out their names.

He learned to forget
his hurt and regret
he walked on his own, legs like two flames.

He grew dirty and tired and thirsty,
at the next town
he decided to stop at the bar.

And he saw then: no matter how far you have come,
you can never be further than right where you are.

These things I know

Language lives when you speak it. Let it be heard.
The worst thing that can happen to words is that they go unsaid.

Let them sing in your ears and dance in your mouth and ache in your
  guts. Let them make everything tighten and shine.

Poetry trembles alone, only picked up to be taken apart.

Instead of an elephant, roaring and shaking its ears,
it's one of those handbag dogs, yapping and scared of the rain.

The clever folk talk in endless circles and congratulate themselves on
  being so untouched by passion.
But since when did the clever folk ever know anything?

Sometimes things *are* as simple as they seem.

It's as much about instinct as it is about intellect
And if you feel it, it's alive.

Let it be magic.
These are not engines we're making.

Wherever you come from is a holy place.

Do not love the idea of life more than you love life itself.

The world is a terrible place for sensitive people
but the closer we come to losing our minds, the harder we'll work
  to keep them.

If you're not fighting for it, you don't want it.

Taking things for granted is a terrible disease. We should all be checking ourselves regularly for signs of it.

Sensitive people are frequently beaten up by things insensitive people can't see.

If you've been beaten up, good for you.
If you've never been beaten up, good for you.
If you get beaten up all the time, you should take up boxing.

It's ok to feel alone.
Usually you are.
That's what poetry's for.

It's good to care about things so much you feel exhausted.

Don't read women's magazines. They're bad for your stomach.

You've only yourself to blame when someone half as talented as you ends up achieving twice as much.

If people judge you badly and misunderstand you,
it's good for you.

Fame is the worst thing that could happen to your reputation.

If you want to know your worth, ask your lovers.
Especially the ones who don't talk to you anymore.

You can't be a good person and treat your lovers badly,
no matter how much you give to charity.

Better to have been a dickhead and seen it,
than be a cunt all your life and not know it.

A thousand fans screaming your name is nothing compared to one
    lover who whispers it and knows what it means.
Although of course both would be nice.

The world is getting stranger every day; you're not strange for
    noticing.

You don't have to be young to be good at what you do. You just have
    to be good at it.

There's nothing wrong with dogs being dogs and baring their teeth
    at each other.

The pain of having fucked things up so bad will never leave us.

If you say something funny on Twitter, it doesn't matter.

If you've been an arsehole today, acknowledge it.
Try not to be one tomorrow.

Never underestimate how nice it is
to make someone a cup of tea without them having to ask.

If you have a shit job and you don't love your girlfriend and your life is killing you, take a fucking risk for once.

If some people don't hate your work, you're not doing it right.

Watching my dog sleep

after Dermot Healy

Murphy is dreaming:
his muscles are twitching,
his ears are alive,
his paws scrape the air.

He's dreaming of yesterday,
stones thrown into waves.
The heartbreak of chasing
what's no longer there.

Learning curve

You taught me what a body's for.
Before you I was scared of being stripped completely naked
even in the throes of it.

I never quite lost myself.
But would watch it from above.
Never so completely moved
that I understood what all the fuss was for.

Since you, I stare unashamedly at strangers.
Hold their eyes for seconds at a time.
Smile like I'd know what to do if they smiled back,
panic when they do.

I am faithful to the lessons you have taught me,
but they've flooded me with hungers I've not satisfied before.
And so I find myself breathless in a Brooklyn tranny bar
stunned by a woman who is kissing me like I am you.

Morning after opening night

So that was it. And it is done,
and now the artist can move on.
Behind him, what he has achieved
is slouching close. Morose, aggrieved.

Most days he can't abide the work,
it spits from every seat.
Most nights, it sends him half berserk
and turns his flesh to meat.

A first night. A public showing,
a winning smile. A finished poem.
Applying perfume to the skin
of all the mess that lives within.

Ideas are such perfect things.
But soon as they're made real
they're cringing, clunky, turgid things,
so difficult to wield.

That's what keeps him trying though;
he'll stare till he's half blind.
It's the search that will define him,
not the thing he's trying to find.

Seeking out a secret in
the light, the rain, the traffic.
A thing that makes him less alone.
Some sudden, brutal magic;

an angel in the takeaway
who floods his veins with sun.
The sentences that strangers say.
A child having fun.

Daylight on a dozing man.
A damp patch on the ceiling.
Anything can shake his hands
and flood his soul with feeling.

And it's worth all the agony,
the wanting to be *more*
for that fickle ecstasy
when he knows what he's for.

That burning punch from paradise
eternal in the moment.
When it's good it's very good,
the rest is all atonement.

Down the pub

It was something about the shape of his face
the size of him. I couldn't take my eyes off him.

I just wanted him to know without me saying
that I needed him to put me in my place.

We were joking, all together, shooting pool.
I was standing, legs apart, smoking fags and swearing.

Beside me, with their slender waists and shipwreck eyes
the girls were dancing, and I was dying

to be like them; until one put her breasts
against my body and my feelings changed.

The point

The days, the days they break to fade.
What fills them I'll forget.
Every touch and smell and taste.
This sun, about to set

can never last. It breaks my heart.
Each joy feels like a threat:
Although there's beauty everywhere,
its shadow is regret.

Still, something in the coming dusk
whispers not to fret.
Don't matter that we'll lose today.
It's not tomorrow yet.

Penance

What you don't know is that
I've written this poem a hundred times,
scribbled it over countless takeaway menus and flyers for shit raves
in the only pen I could ever find,
which was always a miniature turquoise rollerball.

I've found scraps of it in my pockets
and set fire to it on fifteen different windowsills.
And watched the wind catch the ashes
and each time blow them back in my face.

I write it, and imagine giving it to you,
and I get so scared that you will shake your head
and tell me you can't trust a word I say
that I screw it up really small
and wedge it down the back of the bus seats
with the chicken bones.

Man down

Let it be known: no man is entirely alone
No man is a man all through.
I've seen you. Shivering. Fleeting weakness.
Cold rain scuffing its feet on the beaches.
Young human. You. All feeling, flesh.
Brine eyes. Man, but human first.
Stand up. Tall and strong and curved.
Your body makes my body hurt.
A godkid. Perfect. Gloss and dirt.

None of it's real, we are made manifest
By the hearts that bang hard on the bars of our chests –
Let them out.
But we can't though. Too much to lose.
You've got to keep face, keep pace. Keep cool.
And what do I know? You're the man here.
I've got to stop telling you things.
You'll give when you're ready.
I've got to stop wanting.
Your mind's made up.
I've got to stop pushing.
You're trying to keep steady.

No man's too man to hear things.
No tears no tantrums. Resorting to type. So handsome.
No woman's too woman to take it all in.
Quietly solve it, not try and control it,
But fix it so subtle that no one will notice.

Be all that you are, all woman all soft.
All man. All soft. All flesh. All bone. All organ.
I find you more than yourself. I hear you talk to yourself in
    the night-time.
But don't worry, I won't say a word to your friends.

Your voice. Your tears. Your cries. Your panic.
You are more man when you break and weep.
When you shake and sleep,
Body wrapped around your pillow
Safer than a body that bites back.
Your billowing shirt as you sprint through the dirt. Night cap.
One for the road. But the road never loved you.
I love you. I love what you hate in yourself.
It's perfect.
Let it come out.

The best boys would feel like a lady in your arms.
The best girls would fuck like a man, given half the chance.
The good ones are good ones because they are whole ones.
We're at our best when we mean it.
We all start part of a much bigger notion.
And lock ourselves down like we don't have a say.
We come from man and woman combined
And we'll carry those parts till we see our last day.
Hear me. Let it be known.

Your muscles are mine, let's stretch.
Dawn by the bins. We giggle and wretch –
The dawn's on your skin. You're shivering, wet.
You'll cry from your pores if not from your eyes.
Your blood's the same colour as mine.

What a man ever was is enough. It's enough.
Stop trying. Give everything up. No shame here.

No woman's too woman to stand tall and strong.
No man's too man to want loving. Need guidance.
All hearts shrink before violence.
All fists clench for their friends.
We're from here.
We carry it.
Everything that ever went wrong here.
Every single body that gave in.
Caved in.
Break through the boards in the windows.
Find a man thinner than string.
Blinking.
Trying to keep everything in.

Foul smell of the things that we do to escape
There is no glamour in this. No rock and roll.
This is just endings. This is just grief.
And you've got a soul worth living for.
I'm blocking blows for you. But I can't protect you.
I'm too slow for you.
I'm too alive to be near all this death.
I love you. I will not walk off.
But each time my heart falls out of my chest
And sits there, knees pulled up to its chest
It strikes me that there's hardly anything left.

For all of the things that we learnt in this city.
For all of the things that it taught.
You are more than the last pair of trainers you bought.
Never just one thing.
We're all things.
But all things fall short.

A man is a man when he clings to his friends.
A woman's a woman when she holds it down.
A man is a man who takes up her cauldron.
A woman's a woman who takes up his crown.
And wears it for all the right reasons.
And stirs it for all the right reasons.
Humans.
Born with the bodies that need to release.
Find me inside you.
Let me be all that I am.
Tiresias. Wringing my hands.
Tiresias. Singing the hymns of the land.

BLIND PROFIT

TIRESIAS: Where's the glory, killing the dead twice over?

– Sophocles, *Antigone*

The prophet Tiresias

So after all that.
Three lifetimes behind you,
And just at the moment you've found some peace,
You are dragged before the gods,
No mention of the lives you've lived.
The things you've learned to cultivate, like
Living in the moment.

You'd be angry if you weren't so resigned
To letting nothing take you by surprise any longer.

That first dark journey.
Begging your feet to carry you somewhere you might recognise the
    smell of.
The whole world spinning within you.
A darkness. You can't get a breath.
The howling of Hera still sharp in your ears
The feeling of godsized palms on your forehead,
The sudden nausea that trampled your body.

When your eyes began to fog, it was just spots of dark at first,
Expanding out.
Until nothing. Straining to see round the edge of the smudge, through
    the middle or something. Pushing,
But nothing.
While within, another sight, another sense is growing.
Some lightness somewhere.
A feeling of certainty.
The ache of a purpose. The fear. The crippling doubt.
Here it comes.

Ballad of a hero

Your Daddy is a soldier son,
Your Daddy's gone to War,
His steady hands they hold his gun,
His aim is keen and sure.

Your Daddy's in the desert now,
The darkness and the dust,
He's fighting for his country, yes,
He's doing it for us.

Your Daddy's coming home soon though,
Not long now till he's back,
We'll dress you in your smartest shirt
And meet him down the track.

He'll put you on his shoulders and
You'll sing and clap and laugh,
I'll wrap my arms around his waist,
And hold him close at last.

Your Dad ain't left the house again,
Your Dad ain't brushed his teeth,
Your Dad keeps getting angry son,
At nights he doesn't sleep.

He's having his bad dreams again,
He seems worn out and weak,
I've tried to be there for him, but
We barely even speak.

He can't think what to say to me,
He don't know how to tell it,
Won medals for his bravery,
But just wants to forget it.

He's drinking more than ever son,
Before, he never cried.
But now, I wake at night and feel
Him shaking by my side.

He spoke to me at last my son!
He turned to me in tears,
I held him close and kissed his face
And asked him what he feared.

He said *it's getting darker,*
It hasn't disappeared,
And I can see it sharper
Now the sand and smoke have cleared.

There was this kid he'd got to know,
Young boy. Just turned eighteen,
Bright and kind, his name was Joe,
He kept his rifle clean.

Joe's girlfriend was expecting,
Joe loved to joke and laugh,
Joe marched in front of your old man,
As they patrolled a path.

Everything was quiet until
They heard the dreaded blast.
The man that marched in front of Joe
Was completely blown apart.

Some shrapnel hit Joe in the face,
Gouged both eyes at once,
The last thing those eyes ever saw
Was the man in front:

Limbs and flesh and bone and blood,
Torn up and thrown around,
And after that – just blackness.
The taste, the stink, the sound.

I tell you this my son because
I know what you'll be like,
As soon as you've grown old enough
You'll want to go and fight

In whatever battle needs you,
You'll pledge your blood and bone,
Not in the name of good or evil –
But in the name of home.

Your Dad believes in fighting.
He fights for you and I,
But the men that send the armies in
Will never hear him cry.

I don't support the war my son,
I don't believe it's right,
But I do support the soldiers who
Go off to war to fight.

Troops just like your daddy son,
Soldiers through and through,
Who wear their uniform with pride,
And do what they're told to do.

When you're grown, my sweet, my love,
Please don't go fighting wars,
But fight the men that start them
Or fight a cause that's yours.

It seems so full of honour, yes,
So valiant, so bold,
But the men that send the armies in
Send them in for gold,

Or they send them in for oil,
And they tell us it's for Britain
But the men come home like Daddy,
And spend their days just drinking.

Sigh

I saw the best minds of my generation destroyed by payment plans

Progress

Once there was a purpose,
so I hear: there was a God.

It made it all less worthless
and it gave us the because

we'd all been searching for.
An unarguable truth.

A reason to be kind and just,
a reason for the noose

that sent the sinner off to sinnerland
and made us all feel better

in the knowledge that the righteous
would be right and just forever.

Once there was religion, and it ruled.
We had it bad.

We fooled ourselves to sleep at night;
This was This, and That was That.

And if our morals ever shook,
we looked no further than The Book.

But over time we felt the pressure;
it became the great oppressor.

And without God, the wars seemed crueller
life seemed bleaker. Art seemed foolish.

Death seemed stranger now than ever.
What was mankind for? What terror

flooded us to understand
there was no point, no grander plan.

There was just living out each day.
Work. Eat. Sleep. Fuck. Pass away.

Without the fear of retribution
we found guilt-free pleasure

but we lost the sense of union
that had kept us all together.

We needed something new
to fill the emptiness that grew;

and what's better to believe in
than all-you-can-eat Freedom!

The joy of being who we are
by virtue of the clothes we buy.

The dream of getting rich enough
to live outside the common life.

And now, there is no purpose
that exists beyond our needs.

Now there is the worship
of convenience and speed.

We run around the circuit,
pit our grace against our greed

And all we have is surplus
to what's needed and we feed

our callous little urchins
in the best way that we can.

And then wonder how they've grown
to only know what's in their hands.

Now we have the Screen,
and it rules.

Our kids are perma-plugged into its promise,
admiring all its jewels.

And couples eat their dinner,
in the glimmer of its rays,

we stare until
we've learned the world's ways.

Pre-teens learn what heart-throbs are.
Heart-throbs gorge on hot pork and watch sport.

Reality played for us to sneer and weep at –
here is morality at last! See us caught

in full colour, high definition.

Look – a cripple on a blind date.
Look – young people getting fucked in Magaluf,

look – the mother of a dead son, weeping, irate,
look – a celebrity eating shit and singing Agadoo.

We used to burn women who had epileptic fits.
We'd tie them to a stake and proclaim them a witch.

Now

we'll put them on a screen if they've got nice tits,
but they'll be torn apart if they let themselves slip.

We'll draw red rings round their saggy bits.
And flick through the pictures while we eat bags of chips.

You can either be a beauty or a beast or a bitch,
you can either be cool or kooky or kitsch.

Before

you were damned for the things that you did,
or if you didn't live how the villagers lived.

Now

You're handed the mould and told – fit in to this.
And maybe one day you could really be big.

Behind-the-scenes footage
of a famous last gig.

Backstage close-up
of the singer's last twitch.

Before she pulls her gun out
and blows herself to bits.

The world is your playground,
go and get your kicks,

as long as you're not poor,
or ugly, or sick.

We never saw it coming,
like all the best tricks.

Once we had the fear;
now we have the fix.

The downside

They cornered me
and held their knives up to my throat.

They asked me for the football scores.
They asked me for the winning horse.

They asked me for the lotto draw.
Six numbers each and bonus balls.

All I could see
in flickering, ultraviolet pixels

Were their great-grandchildren
ripped to pieces by the missiles

Fine, thanks

To really see the state of things is lethal.
It's safer just to see what we can bear.
Exhausting being fear-struck; howling, weak-willed.
Much nicer to be bathing in the glare

of all that we have built to shine and soothe us
what use are eyes at all in times like this?
Please don't bother raising arms to shoot us,
we'll shoot ourselves. No really, we insist.

No guns. Just give us brands and bills and wages,
and rent that takes our dignity away.
Don't trouble yourselves with handcuffs and with cages.
There's cleaner ways than that to make us pay.

What good can come from listening to our instincts?
You think it's easy putting up like this?
Don't make a fuss, you know us, we're the English,
and peace on Earth won't help us feed our kids.

Our eyes are trained on pinpricks in the blackness.
The telly helps to end a dismal day.
The visions come when we are at our weakest.
But they don't last that long, so it's ok.

Cruise control

The weather will change,
We'll think it malicious.
Speak hurricanes' names and worry in secret.
The waves will build somewhere way out in the ocean,
And flatten whole towns when they break on the beaches.

It won't be enough. We'll plough on
The mightiest we've ever been.
Standing like gods on the shoulders of history.
Or tossing our curls in the sun.

We'll stare down at the screens in our hands
And smile at the photos. *Didn't we laugh.*
Strange voices will sing from street corners.
Powerful men will mumble it into the backs
Of the people they fuck. *This is the end.*

Health and safety slogans will resonate like ancient proverbs.
Don't use the lifts in the case of fire.
Make yourself aware of your nearest exit.
We'll bury our heads in the sand of our lovers.

The waters will boil in the oceans.
Dead things will float on the waves.
The ice caps will thicken to slush puppies
As hurricanes twist
Like boxers in sleeping bags, trying to throw punches.

There'll be fires in the forests, floods in the cities.
And men too rich to swim will die.
The skin on our children will toughen and harden.
And still we will debase ourselves
For that piece of land or mineral
That rock or bomb or golden egg
That might allow one dying person to imagine
They are worth more than another.

And as we followed dinosaurs

Whatever follows us
Will hunt for footprints in the lowlands,
And piece together fragments of our habits
From the internet.

A fossilised smartphone preserved behind glass
For the new young to traipse past on school trips,
Yawning.

Radical empathy

I feel a peace beyond these fumes.
It's coming. I can feel it surging.
Drumming on the curbs, it's burning up,
It's gaining ground.

A peace that we are born deserving.
One we learn to think absurd.
It's in us, or at least, the yearning.
Quickly, stamp it down.

It must be getting nearer.
We can feel it shake within us.
While the echo of each violence done
Pulls out our teeth and breaks our fingers.

Each time you walk the street and flinch
At shadows, see a demon coming,
Visualise your body falling
Under trains or into nothing,
Every time you sense a figure
Running for you, grabbing hold,
To beat you down and leave you dying,
Rob you blind and leave you cold –

It's not the fear or the desire to fall.
It's a memory.
Each wrong is repeated relentlessly.
All thought is eternal.
All life is empathy.

The streets are thick with everything that's ever happened anywhere.
Feel it in the presence of the crowds.
Shouting in your ears when you are bowed and in tears.
It's here.
We can turn our backs forever but we'll never drown it out.

Every time a body's bled its last,
A child dead before it's learned that life is fast,
It stays behind, repeating.
You say you feel the monsters in the dark,
They are not monsters,
They are memories of human things that need to be addressed, appeased.

But there is peace, not heralded by muted brass or soaring strings,
Not worried by the children necking fizzy drinks and sticky wings.
But in us, throbbing, telling us we resolutely must
Not partake in one more horror
If we're to learn to trust.

Fine enough for poets, but in real life
The blood is flowing.
Fine enough to know it,
But it feels like
The love is slowing down,
Getting tired. Cannot lift its weary head.
And all of it continues.
And still nothing can be said.

We are not hateful creatures,
We are good. Our goodness screams for peace.
Everything that's happened can be felt.
Each mouth deserves to speak
Whichever words come to it in the throes of truthful feeling.
But instead
We plunge to numbness.
It's much safer, safety's so appealing

And *what's wrong with wanting comforts?*
My family are worth protecting.
Why should I concern myself with people that I've never met?
And no one's got my back, so why should I have theirs?
My heart throws its head against my ribs,
It's denting every bone it's venting something it has known since I
    arrived and felt it beat.

Party time

He's drunk tonight.
He can't bear another moment
of all day committed to a calling
he never asked for.

He's singing at the roof tops.
Nobody is listening.
He is the old crazy walking into parked cars.

If he sees you strolling home with your arms around each other
he will shout wildly at you and you will smirk knowingly, while you
    try and shake the terror that he's airing your most secret dread.

That deep, raw bark is his calling.
Even tanked up like this, he can't put it out.

Tonight, you see him at a party,
jabbing the air with his fingers,
some kid picked him up on the way over.
Thought it would be funny.

He stands smiling into ears and necks,
dancing like the ancients used to.
But there will come an hour when the dawn is nearly dressed,
when he will start to sway with purpose
and all the laughing kids will hold their sides
and find each other's eyes, like *have you seen this guy*?!
While he bows his head and makes his incantations,
singing like a rabbi.

He's summoning their destinies,
sentencing their spirits;
poor things, the joke's on them –
they think he's rapping lyrics.

Prophet

See him, the old man, blind as our greed,
Alone in the caff with his meat and his gravy.
Witness to every great nation that rose up in hope
And fell prey to itself. *This is slavery.*
Is that what he says to himself? Was it maybe
A mumble that meant something else? Was it *baby*
I miss you? He gets up slow from the table.
Gripping his cane so he's able.

Shuffling, lonesome, sipping black lager,
Park-drunk. Spouting maniacal laughter.
Hard up. Head down. Scarf, gloves, parka.
Every other bastard with a half-arsed grasp on the last judgement is sitting
    in his bathtub
clasping his palms. Each night got his guard up so far that he can't dance
    till he's half-cut.
No damn charm, all they want is to be martyrs.
He spits brown phlegm at the oncoming darkness.

He ridicules grandeur
He understands squalor.
Cake for breakfast.
He can do what he likes.
If these are the last days,
They're no more fast-paced
Than all of the other
Last days and nights.

Buzzwords everywhere. Progress. Freedom.
He picks his teeth with a dirty needle
And kicks his feet to the latest jingles.
Ain't got no time to be dating singles.
Far too busy trying to make things simple.
This old tribe ain't nothing special.
All my life I've watched men wrestle,
Stealing land to fly their flags.
He keeps his eyes in a plastic bag.

He keeps his eyes in a plastic bag.

ACKNOWLEDGEMENTS

Huge thanks to Becky Thomas, Don Paterson
and all at Picador.

'Ballad of a hero' was originally commissioned
by Tongue Fu for The Space and appeared on
thespace.org under the name *War Music* (after Logue).

'I was so much older then, I'm younger than that now'
is a line from Bob Dylan's 'My Back Pages'.

Extract from 'How To Be A Great Writer' from
Love is a Dog From Hell by Charles Bukowski
(Ecco Books) © The Charles Bukowski Estate.

KATE TEMPEST was born in 1985 and grew up in South-East London, where she still lives. She started out as a rapper, toured the spoken word circuit for a number of years and began writing for theatre in 2012. Her work includes the album *Balance*, recorded with Sound of Rum; *Everything Speaks in its Own Way*, a collection of poems published on her own imprint Zingaro; *GlassHouse*, a forum theatre play for Cardboard Citizens; and the plays *Wasted* and *Hopelessly Devoted* for Paines Plough, both published by Methuen. Her epic narrative poem *Brand New Ancients* won the Ted Hughes Prize in 2013; it completed a sell-out run in the UK and New York and won a Herald Angel at Edinburgh Fringe. *Everybody Down*, her debut solo album, was released on Big Dada Records in 2014.